Gloopy Food

Written by Michaela Morgan
Illustrated by Andy Elkerton

Horribilly is a ...

BIG...

green and gloopy...

soggy...

monster.

He is the only monster at Golden Pond School.

Horribilly has lots of friends.

They have lots of fun at school.

"What do you want to eat?"
said his friends at lunch.

Horribilly said,

"Bugs!
I love bugs.
Big and yummy bugs.
I love bugs."

Everyone said, "YUCK!"

"We will help you," said his friends.
They gave him ...

one little pizza,

some fresh salad,

two small bananas

and a brown roll.

This did NOT look
like food to Horribilly.

So, he put the salad in his hair.

He threw the bananas in the air.

He made a frisbee with the pizza.
“Don’t be silly, Horribilly!” said his friends.

Then Horribilly put
the pizza on his nose.

He put the brown roll
on his toes.

He put a banana
in each ear and ...

with the roll
he kicked a goal!

"Don't play with your food!"
said his friends.
"Eat it!"
"It's too dry!" said Horribilly.
"I like gloopy food."

Big, green tears ran down his face.

Then he found tomato sauce.

Now he loves his school lunch ...

and he thinks that bananas are yummy!